MW00344919

# Let My People Laugh

## Other Lillenas Drama Resources by Martha Bolton

*A Funny Thing Happened to Me on My Way Through the Bible*

•

*A View from the Pew*

•

*What's Growing Under Your Bed?*

•

*Tangled in the Tinsel*

•

*The "How'd I Get to Be in Charge of the Program?" Help Book*

# Let My People Laugh

## More Sketches and Monologues
## Based on Familiar Bible Stories

by Martha Bolton

Author of the original *A Funny Thing Happened to Me
on My Way Through the Bible*

A Lillenas Drama Resource

**Lillenas Publishing Company**
**Kansas City, MO 64141**

All rights reserved.

Printed in the United States of America.

Amateur performance rights are granted with your purchase of this book.

You may duplicate individual sketch scripts from this book for $1.00 per copy —$10.00 maximum payment per individual sketch. Please include the following on each reproduced copy:

From *Let My People Laugh*
Copyright © 1989 by Lillenas Publishing Co.
All rights reserved.
Reproduced with permission of Lillenas Publishing Co.

Repro rights are granted upon the receipt of your check along with this information:

1. title of book
2. title of sketch
3. number of copies made

Mail this information with your check to:

Lillenas Drama Resources
Copyright Permission Desk
P.O. Box 419527
Kansas City, MO 64141

Cover art: Crandall Vail
Illustration: Keith Alexander

# Dedication

In memory of my dear friend,
BILL HOEST
May his love and laughter
live on through his work.

# Contents

# Preface

*Let My People Laugh* takes up where *A Funny Thing Happened to Me on My Way Through the Bible* leaves off.

From Adam and Eve's "A Change of Address" to Joseph's "Keep Looking Up—Even When Your Life's in the Pits," the sketches and monologues contained here are easy to perform and easy to direct. Hopefully, though, their messages won't be easy to forget.

So, have fun with them, and remember, sometimes laughter really is the best teacher!

—MARTHA BOLTON

# Acknowledgments

A special thanks . . .

> **To my husband, Russ,** who always encouraged me to pursue a literary career. (At least, I think that's what he meant when he'd show me the door and say, "Don't forget to write!")

> **To my sons, Rusty, Matt, and Tony,** who have had to face some real trials in life. (But, hey, I don't cook *every* meal!)

> **To my dear friend and editor, Paul Miller.** May our fax machines continue to communicate for many years to come!

> **And finally, to those of you** who've expressed appreciation for my books. If you hadn't taken the time to write, I would never have known what great paperweights they make!

# A Change of Address

## A sketch about Adam and Eve

**Characters:**
> ADAM
> EVE

**Setting:**
> Just outside the Garden of Eden

**Props:**
> Various plants, bushes, etc.

**Costumes:**
> ADAM: leaf shirt and pants
> EVE: leaf dress

*(Sketch opens with* ADAM *and* EVE *as they're leaving the Garden of Eden.)*

EVE: Don't say it!

ADAM: I told you so.

EVE: I told you not to say it!

ADAM: Well, why couldn't you leave well enough alone, Eve? We had a beautiful home in the garden. We had all the food we wanted. No bills. No traffic jams. No door-to-door salesmen. No worries. But noooooo! You had to have more! You had to eat of the forbidden fruit!

EVE: Hey, if I've said it once, I've said it a hundred times, the serpent tempted me.

ADAM: So? You couldn't just say no?

EVE: Well, you ate some, too, you know.

ADAM: I was merely trying to dispose of the evidence.

EVE *(sarcastic):* Yeah. Right.

ADAM: And anyway, you're the one who gave us away.

EVE: How do you figure that?

ADAM: God heard you say, "I don't have a thing to wear!"

EVE: I'm a woman. It seemed like a natural thing to say.

ADAM: But if you hadn't eaten the fruit, you wouldn't have known your wardrobe was lacking.

EVE: Look, Adam, God knew we had disobeyed Him before I said a word. He's God. He knows everything.

ADAM: Well, all I know is one of us has to start looking for a nine-to-five now, so which way's the Unemployment Office?

EVE: Hey, I'm not happy about any of this either, you know. Because of our sin, God said we're gonna have to start living off the land now. . . . You think I wanna cook?!

ADAM: That reminds me, what's for dinner?

EVE: I've been under so much stress today, can't we just order take-out?

ADAM: Take-out? But we're the only people on earth!

EVE: Good. There won't be any orders ahead of us!

ADAM *(losing patience):* Eve, get out the Crock pot and get busy!

EVE: All right, but if I have to cook dinner, then you take out the garbage! *(She starts gathering nearby leaves, etc., for dinner.)*

ADAM *(unimpressed with her choice of ingredients):* Maybe I should wait. They could turn out to be the same thing!

EVE *(glares at him for a moment, then smiles):* Look, why are we arguing? What's done is done. We'll just have to make the best of our new home.

ADAM: You're right, Eve. And when we have children, we'll have to teach them how important it is to obey God.

EVE: . . . because disobedience will always cost more than you think.

ADAM: Now, let's get that grub on the table!

EVE: OK, but you'd better remember this night.

ADAM: Why's that?

EVE: It's the only night in history where a wife couldn't cook leftovers! *(As they both continue to gather leaves, etc., go to blackout.)*

# The Happy Parents
## or
## "We're Gonna Have a *What?*"

---

## A sketch about Abraham and Sarah

---

**Characters:**
> ABRAHAM
> SARAH

**Setting:**
> Their home

**Props:**
> None needed

**Costumes:**
> Bible era clothing

*(Sketch opens with* SARAH *and* ABRAHAM *standing center stage, discussing the good news.)*

SARAH: We're gonna have a *what?*

ABRAHAM: A baby! An angel of the Lord came and told me we were going to have a baby!

SARAH: I know. I overheard you talking with him, but I thought my ears were playing tricks on me.

ABRAHAM: They're not playing tricks. God is going to bless us with a child. Isn't it wonderful, Sarah?

SARAH: But Abraham, you're 99, and I'm . . . I'm . . . well, let's just say I'm not a teenager anymore.

ABRAHAM: You're 90.

SARAH: So, I rest my case! How can we have a baby at our age?

ABRAHAM: Is anything too hard for the Lord?

SARAH: No. But a baby, Abraham? Do you know what this means? We'll be the oldest parents at Open House.

ABRAHAM: It means we'll be a testimony of God's faithfulness! Now, c'mon, admit it, Sarah. You're just as excited as I am!

SARAH: Of course, I'm excited. I've always wanted a child, but at our age, it just seemed impossible.

ABRAHAM: Our God is a God of the impossible, Sarah.

SARAH: I'm finding that out! . . . Well, now, let's see, there are so many things we must do! We'll have to fix up the nursery—pink curtains, pink dressing table, a cute little pink lamp . . .

ABRAHAM: I don't think Isaac's gonna be that fond of pink.

SARAH: We can't name our daughter "Isaac"! Her friends will make fun of her.

ABRAHAM: We're not having a daughter, Sarah. We're having a son.

SARAH: A son? That's even better news! But how do you know that?

ABRAHAM: The Lord told me, and He said we're to call him "Isaac."

SARAH: Then, blue curtains it is! . . . You know, Abraham, who would have thought two people our age could be having a baby!

ABRAHAM: Happy Mother's Day, Sarah.

SARAH: I've waited 90 years to hear someone say that. And you know what?

ABRAHAM: What?

SARAH: It sounds even better than I imagined! God is good and faithful to His promises, isn't He, Abraham?

ABRAHAM: That He is, Sarah, that He is!

(Blackout.)

# A Wedding Surprise

## A sketch about Jacob and Leah

**Characters:**
> MINISTER
> JACOB
> LEAH

**Setting:**
> Wedding chapel

**Props:**
> Ceremony book

**Costumes:**
> MINISTER: suit or Bible era costume of clergy
> JACOB: appropriate groom's attire, Bible times
> LEAH: appropriate bride's attire with veil, Bible times

**Sound Effects:**
> Organ music

*(Sketch opens with* JACOB *and* LEAH *standing before* MINISTER. *The ceremony book is in his hand.* LEAH's *veil is over her face, so* JACOB *can't really see her.)*

MINISTER: I pronounce you husband and wife. Jacob, you may now kiss your bride.

JACOB *(lifts veil and starts to kiss her, then stops abruptly)*: Hey, wait a minute! This isn't the woman I thought I was marrying!

MINISTER: Are they ever?

JACOB: No, I mean, this isn't Rachel. It's Leah, her older sister.

MINISTER: Well, at least it's in the same family since her father, Laban, already got stuck with the catering bill.

JACOB: But I made a deal with Laban to work for him seven years in exchange for the hand of his daughter, Rachel, not Leah.

LEAH: Look, tradition has it the oldest daughter must marry first. You can't just take your pick. This isn't "The Love Connection," you know.

JACOB: Then why did the wedding announcements say "Rachel and Jacob"? Why do the napkins say "Rachel and Jacob"? Why does the cake say "Rachel and Jacob"?

LEAH: Can I help it if the wedding consultant didn't know how to spell?

MINISTER: Look, Jacob, what's done is done. Maybe you should just try to make the best of it.

JACOB: You mean I worked those seven years for nothing?

LEAH: You can learn to love me, Jacob. I'm a good cook, an excellent housekeeper, and I never watch soap operas.

JACOB: But I love Rachel. Why, she's the most beautiful girl I've ever laid my eyes upon.

LEAH: And what am I? A sheep decoy?

JACOB: You're pretty, too, Leah. It's just that I had always planned for Rachel to be my wife.

MINISTER: Maybe you can work out another deal with Laban. You know, work another seven years in exchange for Rachel.

JACOB: Another 7 years?! That'd be a total of 14 years of labor just for one woman!

MINISTER: And that's not even counting all the jobs she'll have for you to do *after* you get married!

JACOB (*thinks for a moment*): Ah, but Rachel's worth it! . . . All right, I guess I'll do it. But I still say this was pretty sneaky!

LEAH: About as sneaky as the trick you played on your father, Isaac, to get the birthright away from your brother?

JACOB (*surprised, then embarrassed*): OK, you've got me there. I guess he who deceives others shouldn't be surprised when he gets deceived himself.

MINISTER: I couldn't have said it better myself!

(*As the organist plays a suitable wedding recessional,* JACOB *reservedly holds his arm out for* LEAH. *She takes it, and the newlyweds exit, arm in arm.*)

(*Blackout.*)

# Keep Looking Up— Even When Your Life's in the Pits

## A monologue about Joseph

**Character:**
> JOSEPH

**Setting:**
> The pit

**Props:**
> None needed

**Costume:**
> Bible time clothes (Joseph should not be wearing the coat of many colors, as this was taken from him before being thrown into the pit.)

*(Monologue opens with* JOSEPH *in the pit. He calls out to his brothers.)*

OK, you guys. The joke's over. It was funny for a while, but now, c'mon, get me out of here. This place is dingy, dusty, and unfit for human inhabitants. . . . You know, like a teenager's bedroom.

Now, enough is enough. Lower down a rope. It'll be dark soon, and I need to be getting back. Father will be worried.

*(Cupping his hand over his mouth)* Hello! Can you hear me up there?

Look, I know you've never been real fond of me. You got mad when I told you my dreams. And you were always jealous of my coat of many colors. But is that any reason to do this? To leave me in this pit all alone . . . in the wilderness . . . on a cold night . . . with wild beasts running loose? *(He listens briefly for an answer, but there is none.)* Umphf! Well, all I've got to say is this is sure gonna cost you some points for the "Brothers of the Year Award."

And just remember, someday *you're* gonna be hungry and cold and in desperate need, and who will *you* come to for help? Me! That's who!

And will I help you? Will I feed you? Will I forgive my brothers after they've done such evil to me? *(He thinks for a moment, then thoughtfully . . .)* Of course, I will. You know why? Because I realize my life may be in the pits today, but if I keep looking up, God will lift me up to higher places. In fact, He might even have a room already reserved for me in some palace somewhere.

So, go ahead, do what you must. But I'm trusting God to turn your evil into good. And who knows, maybe someday soon I'll get the chance to show you what being a brother is really all about.

*(Blackout.)*

# They Went Thataway

## A sketch about the parting of the Red Sea

**Characters:**

ZAPANEAH ⎫
⎬ Two members of Pharaoh's army
NEPHRAIM ⎭

**Setting:**

The banks of the Red Sea

**Props:**

None needed

**Costume:**

Egyptian army attire from that era (capes, headgear, sandals, etc.)

*(We open with* ZAPANEAH *and* NEPHRAIM *standing center stage.)*

ZAPANEAH *(frustrated):* All right, so *now* what do we do?

NEPHRAIM: We follow them.

ZAPANEAH: Follow them? But Moses and the Israelites just marched through the Red Sea on dry ground! Do you have any idea what that means?

NEPHRAIM: They have a better travel agent than us?

ZAPANEAH: It means the God they serve is one powerful God!

NEPHRAIM: Look, all I know is that we have our orders from Pharaoh. Now, c'mon, after those Israelites!

ZAPANEAH: Right! *(He starts to go, then stops.)* Wait a minute. Where are my manners? You go first.

NEPHRAIM: No, no. I wouldn't think of it. You go first.

ZAPANEAH: No, please, after you.

NEPHRAIM: No. After you.

ZAPANEAH: You're stalling.

NEPHRAIM: *You're* stalling.

ZAPANEAH: But what if the walls of water don't hold up for us? We could find ourselves at the bottom of the sea, you know.

NEPHRAIM: So? Isn't that how you usually swim anyway?

ZAPANEAH: I've got it! We'll tell Pharaoh our chariots ran out of gas!

NEPHRAIM: Chariots don't run on gas.

ZAPANEAH: OK. We'll say our horses ran out of gas.

NEPHRAIM: Horses don't run on gas either.

ZAPANEAH (*thinks for a moment*): No wonder everyone was looking at me funny at the filling station!

NEPHRAIM (*losing his patience*): Look, how 'bout if we both go at the same time?

ZAPANEAH: I guess that sounds fair. (*They take a few steps forward, then he trips.*) Uh-oh, I think I just sprained my ankle. You'll have to go on without me.

NEPHRAIM: Nice try, O'Chicken of the Red Sea! Now, get movin'! They're getting away!

ZAPANEAH: OK (*takes a few steps, then stops again*), but did I happen to mention these are my good sandals?

NEPHRAIM (*ordering*): Forward! March!

ZAPANEAH: All right, all right, I'm going, I'm going. (*He starts to walk forward.*) But answer me this, will ya? What is it about these Israelites that makes Pharaoh want them back so badly?

NEPHRAIM: I think it's some kind of macho thing. Pharaoh's trying to prove he won't be pushed around by the God of the Israelites.

ZAPANEAH: But their God's already sent 10 plagues upon Egypt and now He's parted the Red Sea for them. Doesn't Pharaoh know when he's licked?

NEPHRAIM: Apparently not. Now, after those Israelites!

(*They start to run, but once again* ZAPANEAH *stops.*)

ZAPANEAH: Just one more thing . . .

NEPHRAIM: *Now* what is it?

ZAPANEAH: Well *(looking off into the distance)*, it appears the last Israelite has just stepped safely onto the shore on the other side.

NEPHRAIM: Yeah. So?

ZAPANEAH: So, what if that's all their God was waiting for?

NEPHRAIM: What do you mean?

ZAPANEAH: What if He was just waiting for His people to cross safely, and then . . .

NEPHRAIM: Yes?

ZAPANEAH: And then . . .

NEPHRAIM *(anxious):* And then *what?*

ZAPANEAH *(pointing upward):* Surf's up.

NEPHRAIM *(panicked):* Oh, no! The wall of water's giving way! We're all gonna drown!

ZAPANEAH: Would this be a good time to say "I told you so"?

NEPHRAIM: Just do me one favor, will ya?

ZAPANEAH: What's that?

NEPHRAIM: The next time Pharaoh decides to take on the God of the Israelites . . .

ZAPANEAH: Yeah?

NEPHRAIM: Remind me to go A.W.O.L.!

(ZAPANEAH *nods, and they both mime a few swimming strokes as they exit offstage.)*

*(Blackout.)*

# They Were So Big . . .

## A sketch about the two faithful spies

**Characters:**
CALEB
SHAPHAT
IGAL

**Setting:**
Outside the Promised Land

**Props:**
None needed

**Costumes:**
Bible era clothing

*(Sketch opens with* CALEB, SHAPHAT, *and* IGAL *gathered together talking.)*

CALEB: Well, isn't Canaan everything God said it would be?

SHAPHAT: That it is! And then some!

CALEB: Then, I say we go in and take it! What are we waiting for?

IGAL: For one thing, our knees to stop shaking!

SHAPHAT: Caleb, didn't you see the size of those Canaanites? Those dudes have been taking their vitamins!

CALEB: They weren't so big.

IGAL: Are you kidding? The ark could have been their bath toy!

CALEB: But my brothers, you're not looking at the positives.

SHAPHAT: Sure, we are. We're positive we're *not* going in!

CALEB: But I know we can bring the Canaanites to their knees!

IGAL: Yeah, and they'd *still* be taller than us! Why, next to those Canaanites, we look as small as grasshoppers!

CALEB: The only thing small is your faith.

SHAPHAT: I'd go in a second, Caleb, but it's my feet. Lately, I've been having problems with them.

CALEB: Really?

SHAPHAT: Yeah, every time I come against an enemy this big, they want to turn around and run!

IGAL: Well, what about me? Don't forget I've got a wife and mother-in-law at home.

CALEB: And you don't think you should leave them?

IGAL: No. I was hoping they could go in my place!

CALEB *(frustrated)*: OK—so maybe the Canaanites *are* bigger than us. And maybe they're tougher. But you're forgetting one thing. God is on our side!

SHAPHAT: Yes, but . . .

CALEB: Didn't He free us from Pharaoh's bondage?

SHAPHAT: Well, yes . . .

CALEB: And didn't He part the Red Sea?

IGAL: Yes . . .

CALEB: And didn't He feed us with manna every day?

SHAPHAT: Yes . . .

CALEB: Then I say we can trust Him for this! And Joshua agrees with me!

(SHAPHAT *and* IGAL *briefly confer.*)

SHAPHAT: OK, Caleb, we've talked it over, and there was one question we just had to ask ourselves—are we mice or men?

CALEB *(encouraged)*: And your answer?

IGAL AND SHAPHAT *(together)*: Got any cheese?

CALEB: All right, go ahead. Stay here and look at the negatives. Live in fear. Don't take that which the Lord has given to you. But I know one day Joshua and I will march triumphant into the Promised Land!

SHAPHAT: But what about the Canaanites? You'll still look like grasshoppers next to them.

CALEB: Maybe. But we're two grasshoppers who serve a mighty big God!

*(Blackout.)*

# The Donkey Who Had Something to Say

---

## A sketch about Balaam and the donkey

---

**Characters:**
> Clerk
> Balaam
> Soldier

**Setting:**
> Animal Behavior School

**Props:**
> Counter
> Pad and pen
> Sign that says "Animal Behavior School"
> Ice pack

**Costumes:**
> Clerk: business suit
> Balaam: Bible era clothing and bandage on foot
> Soldier: soldier attire from Bible times

(*Sketch opens with* Clerk *behind the counter, trying desperately to get* Balaam's *story straight. The pen is in her hand, the pad of paper in front of her. The sign, "Animal Behavior School," is in full view of the audience. The ice pack is not.*)

CLERK: Now, tell me again, sir, why have you brought your donkey to us?

BALAAM: He's been acting a little strange lately.

CLERK: Well, now, many animals do things that may seem strange to us, but are, in fact, perfectly normal for them. So, why don't you tell me what it is your donkey did, and let a professional make the final judgment?

BALAAM: He talked to me.

CLERK: He talked to you? (BALAAM *nods.*) Excuse me, sir, but I believe you've accidentally stumbled into the wrong office. "House of Nuts" is two doors down. Good day.

BALAAM: But I'm telling you the truth!

CLERK: Look, Mr. . . . ?

BALAAM: Balaam. B-A-L-A-A-M.

CLERK: Mr. Balaam, I run a legitimate business here. You want your animal to behave himself? Bring him to me. You want him to have better diction, more voice control, greater stage presence? Sign him up in Toastmasters!

BALAAM: You don't believe me, do you?

CLERK: Of course, I do. And Elvis is my stockboy.

BALAAM: Madam, I assure you I am a highly respected man in my community and abroad. I would never joke about something like this.

CLERK (*thinks for a moment*): All right, but maybe you'd better start at the beginning.

BALAAM: Well, you see, I was on my way to see King Balak, the king of the Moabites. He wanted me to put a curse on the Israelites, so he sent his messengers to offer me gifts and to urge me to go to him.

CLERK: And that's when your donkey talked?

BALAAM: Not yet. I knew God didn't want me to curse the Israelites, but I tried asking Him just one more time if I could go ahead and go with the messengers to King Balak. God finally agreed I could go, but I had to only do what He told me.

CLERK: And that's when your donkey talked?

BALAAM: No, not yet. So, I rode away with the men, but then, all of a sudden, my donkey turned off the road and started running across the field.

CLERK: And he talked?

BALAAM: No. I hit him and got him back on the road, but then a short while later, as we were going through a narrow passageway, the donkey pushed up against the wall, crushing my foot.

CLERK: And he said . . . ?

BALAAM: Nothing yet. After I hit him, though, he did start going again. Then, without any warning whatsoever, he just sits down right there in the middle of the road and refuses to go!

CLERK: So you hit him again?

BALAAM: How'd you know?

CLERK: Lucky guess.

BALAAM: Well, *that's* when he talked!

CLERK: What'd he say? "Hit me again and you're history"?

BALAAM: Close. He said, "What have I done to make you beat me three times?" And I said, "You've made fun of me! In fact, if I had a sword right now, I'd probably kill you!"

CLERK: You just started talking to the donkey, simple as that?

BALAAM: Hey, I wasn't about to let him have the last word!

CLERK: So, then what happened?

BALAAM: So, then he said, "I've been your donkey for many years. Have I ever acted like this before?"

CLERK: He had you there, huh?

BALAAM (*nods*): Then, when I looked up, I saw why he'd been acting so strangely. There was an angel with a sword standing before us, blocking the passage.

CLERK: I take it this angel wanted you to turn back.

BALAAM: No, he just wanted to remind me to only do what God told me to do.

CLERK: So you proceeded on your journey?

BALAAM: That's right.

CLERK: And did the animal talk anymore?

BALAAM: Not really. I guess he had already gotten everything off his chest.

CLERK: So, then, did you curse the Israelites?

BALAAM: I tried, but each time I opened my mouth, only good things would come out. I ended up giving them a blessing instead!

CLERK: But I still don't understand what you want me to do? Obviously, it was God who made your donkey speak. So, unless you try to harm the Israelites again, I don't think you'll have to worry about any more speeches from your beast of burden.

BALAAM: Worry about it? I was hoping you could get him to do it again! King Balak refused to give me any of the gifts he had promised because I couldn't curse the Israelites, but hey, a talking donkey could bring me a fortune!

CLERK: Mr. Balaam, didn't you learn anything from your experience?

BALAAM: Sure. I learned to always ask for the gifts in advance!

CLERK: No, I mean didn't you learn something about the God of the Israelites?

BALAAM: Like what?

CLERK: Like He'll go to great extremes to protect His children . . . even if it means making an animal talk. Good day, Mr. Balaam.

BALAAM (*slightly embarrassed by his greed, but not totally repentant*): Good day. (*Exits.*)

CLERK (*calling out to waiting room, offstage*): Next!

(SOLDIER *enters.*)

SOLDIER: Hello.

CLERK: So, tell me, what kind of animal behavior problem are you experiencing?

SOLDIER: Well, you see, I'm in charge of the lions' den for King Darius, and the other day we threw this guy named Daniel in. But instead of eating him, the lions just lay there, calm as you please.

CLERK: Hold it! Don't say another word! . . . By any chance, does this guy, Daniel, serve the God of the Israelites?

SOLDIER: Well, yes, as a matter of fact, he does!

CLERK (*brings ice pack out from behind counter and places it on her head*): Something tells me it's gonna be one of those days!

(*Blackout.*)

# The Right Prescription

## A sketch about Naaman, the leper

**Characters:**
>   NAAMAN
>   NAAMAN'S SERVANT
>   ELISHA'S SERVANT

**Setting:**
>   In front of Elisha's home

**Props:**
>   None needed

**Costumes:**
>   Bible era clothing

*(Sketch opens with* NAAMAN, NAAMAN'S SERVANT, *and* ELISHA'S SERVANT *standing center stage. Obviously,* ELISHA'S SERVANT *has just informed* NAAMAN *of Elisha's strange request.)*

NAAMAN: He wants me to do *what?*

ELISHA'S SERVANT: Wash seven times in the River Jordan.

NAAMAN: But I have leprosy, not a dry skin problem!

ELISHA'S SERVANT: Hey, I'm only the messenger, but I do know one thing. If I had leprosy and Elisha told me to take seven dips in the Jordan River, I'd sure do it.

NAAMAN: But I'm a highly respected captain in the Syrian army. If people see me dipping seven times in the Jordan River, they'll think I've got combat fatigue!

ELISHA'S SERVANT: They may think you're a little strange the first six times, but when you come up that seventh time, they're gonna know you're a guy who sure knows where to put his trust!

NAAMAN *(thinks for a moment)*: How 'bout if I give a large donation to the poor instead?

ELISHA'S SERVANT: The poor will appreciate your generosity, you'll have a nice write-off for your income tax, but you'll still have your leprosy.

NAAMAN: But there are rivers in my own country. What's so special about the Jordan?

ELISHA'S SERVANT: Nothing 'til you obey God and get in it.

NAAMAN *(thinking):* I don't know. It just seems too easy.

NAAMAN'S SERVANT *(to* NAAMAN*):* Master, if this prophet, Elisha, would give you some great thing to do, you'd do it, right?

NAAMAN: Of course, I would! Why, I'd do the most difficult task if it meant this awful plague would leave my body.

NAAMAN'S SERVANT: Then why not do this simple thing? You've nothing to lose.

NAAMAN *(brief pause):* You know, you just might have a point there. *(To* ELISHA'S SERVANT*)* Sir, which way to the Jordan?

ELISHA'S SERVANT *(smiling):* Just stay on this road! You can't miss it!

NAAMAN: Thanks! *(As they turn to leave)* We'll let you know how it turns out.

ELISHA'S SERVANT: No need to do that, sir. I already know how it's going to turn out.

NAAMAN: You do?

ELISHA'S SERVANT: Sure! When Elisha's God is called in on a case, you can rest assured the patient's in the very best of hands!

*(Blackout.)*

# A Whale of a Book Tour

## A sketch about Jonah and the whale

**Characters:**
> LIPS WAGNER
> BIG FISH

**Setting:**
> "The Lips Wagner Talk Show"

**Props:**
> Two chairs
> Desk
> Two microphones
> Hardback book titled *It Must Have Been Something I Ate*

**Costumes:**
> LIPS: Business suit
> BIG FISH: Whale costume*
>     *with sunglasses

*(Sketch opens with* LIPS WAGNER *sitting behind desk. The other chair is to the side of the desk, facing the audience. The book is on the desk.)*

LIPS *(to audience)*: Over the years I've had a lot of people on my talk show who were all wet, but my next guest has reason to be. You've been reading about him in all the major newspapers: The Joppa *Journal*, The Tarshish *Times*, Nineveh *News and World Report*. You've seen him on leading talk shows. And his new book *(holding it up)*, *It Must Have Been Something I Ate*, just made the best-seller list. Ladies and gentlemen, let's give a real Lips Wagner welcome to the most famous marine animal in all of history . . . the fish who swallowed Jonah! *(He rises and leads the audience in applause as* BIG FISH *enters and they both take their seat.)* It was so nice of you to take a few moments out of your busy schedule to be on our show.

BIG FISH: Well, I . . . uh, which way is the camera? *(He removes his sunglasses and looks around a bit.)* Ah, there we go . . . *(He mugs a bit for the camera.)* . . . Now, where were we? . . . Oh, yes, I was about to say that I believe it's time the world heard my side of the whale and Jonah story.

LIPS: Don't you mean "Jonah and the whale"?

BIG FISH: Why should he always get top billing?

LIPS: Well, look, why don't you go ahead and tell our viewers everything that happened on that unforgettable night.

BIG FISH: Very well. You see, I was swimming along minding my own business, when all of a sudden this great storm came up. Now, I've seen great storms before—I'm married—but I've never seen one like this.

LIPS: Then what happened?

BIG FISH: Well, then I noticed these men tossing some things over the side of their boat.

LIPS: What kinds of things?

BIG FISH: Junk, mostly. I guess they were trying to lighten their load. But then, I see them throw something a little more interesting overboard.

LIPS: Jonah?

BIG FISH: Jonah to you. Sunday brunch to me. So, naturally, I raced over there and . . . *(pats stomach)* . . . well the rest is in my book.

LIPS: C'mon, you can tell us. You swallowed Jonah, didn't you?

BIG FISH: I don't know why I did it. I wasn't even hungry that day. But something just made me open my mouth, and the next thing I knew I was harboring a fugitive.

LIPS: So then what happened?

BIG FISH: Well, I was fine for about three days. Then, I started to get this real queasy feeling in the pit of my stomach.

LIPS: And you figured it was Jonah?

BIG FISH: Who else would be pounding on my rib cage shouting, "I should have gone to Nineveh! I should have gone to Nineveh!"?

LIPS: So, that's when you coughed him up?

BIG FISH: No. First, I tried swallowing a couple of life preservers. . . . I thought they were giant antacids. But when that didn't work, I had no choice but to let him go.

LIPS: In other words, it was as though the same thing that made you swallow Jonah made you let him go after three days?

BIG FISH: Exactly. And I know what that something was. It was the Lord.

LIPS: Well, why do you suppose God chose you to help get Jonah back on the right track?

BIG FISH: He's seen what I eat. I guess He figured three days in my stomach would get anybody back on the right track!

LIPS: And how does it feel to know you were instrumental in seeing the entire city of Nineveh repent and be spared destruction?

BIG FISH: Lips, I'm just glad I was there in the right place at the right time to be used of the Lord.

LIPS: Well, listen, it's been a pleasure having you on my show. I know you have more appearances to make today, but before you go, is there one last thought you'd like to leave with our viewers?

BIG FISH: Yes, as a matter of fact, I do have one. When the Lord tells you to do something, do it! Take it from me, running away from God will only get you in deep water! *(He rises to leave.)*

LIPS *(rising):* Ladies and gentlemen, the fish who swallowed Jonah! *(He leads the audience in applause as* BIG FISH *exits, waving. Once again, he lifts the book from the desk and shows it to the audience.)* And don't forget to pick up your copy of *It Must Have Been Something I Ate* at your local bookstore. Available soon in paperback!

*(Blackout.)*

# Keeping Your Cool in a Heated Situation

## A sketch about Shadrach, Meshach, and Abednego

**Characters:**
> REPORTER
> KING NEBUCHADNEZZAR

**Setting:**
> In front of the fiery furnace

**Props:**
> Hand-held microphone

**Costume:**
> REPORTER: Business suit
> NEBUCHADNEZZAR: Kingly attire

*(Sketch opens with* REPORTER *standing center stage with microphone in his hand. He looks out toward audience as if speaking into a television camera.)*

REPORTER: Good evening. This is the "Babylon News and Empire Report." We're here on location in Babylon where three young men have just been thrown into the fiery furnace by order of King Nebuchadnezzar. Let's see if we can get a bit closer. *(He takes a few steps forward but is obviously held back due to the intense heat.)* Uh . . . on second thought, that fire's pretty hot. Maybe I'd better stay back here and hang onto my eyebrows a little longer! *(Looks off to the side.)* But wait! Here comes the king now. *(Calling out)* King Nebuchadnezzar! King Nebuchadnezzar!

NEBUCHADNEZZAR *(enters):* Yes?

REPORTER: King Nebuchadnezzar, is it true you sentenced three young men to die in the fiery furnace today?

NEBUCHADNEZZAR: They disobeyed my decree. When the music was played, they refused to bow down and worship the golden statue. So I did what any other king would do.

REPORTER: You threw them into the fiery furnace?

NEBUCHADNEZZAR: Of course not. I'm a kind, gentle, loving king. I had my guards do it.

REPORTER: I see. Well, perhaps we could speak with these guards.

NEBUCHADNEZZAR: I don't really think they're in the mood. For some reason they got a little burned up over this whole ordeal.

REPORTER: They thought you were too hard on the prisoners, huh?

NEBUCHADNEZZAR: No, I mean they really burned up. You see, I had them turn up the fire seven times hotter than usual.

REPORTER: Seven times! That's pretty hot!

NEBUCHADNEZZAR: Let's just say if you wanted to roast a hot dog, you could do it from a different time zone! Anyway, when they opened the furnace to toss the prisoners in, they caught on fire themselves.

REPORTER: My, my, that's quite a . . . *(He looks toward the furnace, puzzled.)* Uh, sir . . .

NEBUCHADNEZZAR: Yes?

REPORTER: Excuse me, sir, but I thought there were only three prisoners cast into the fiery furnace.

NEBUCHADNEZZAR: That's right. Shadrach, Meshach, and Abednego.

REPORTER: You're sure?

NEBUCHADNEZZAR: Of course, I'm sure.

REPORTER: No one else went in there with them?

NEBUCHADNEZZAR: This isn't exactly the number one tourist attraction of Babylon, you know. What are you driving at?

REPORTER: Well, maybe you'd better take another look.

(REPORTER *steps aside and* NEBUCHADNEZZAR *mimes looking inside the furnace. As he looks, he counts on his fingers: 1, 2, 3, then pauses briefly, 4. He shakes his head, rubs his eyes, and counts again: 1, 2, 3, brief pause, 4.)*

NEBUCHADNEZZAR *(shaking his head)*: Impossible!

REPORTER: Four, right?

NEBUCHADNEZZAR: But only three men, bound and fully clothed, were thrown into this fiery furnace.

REPORTER: Well, now they've got company.

NEBUCHADNEZZAR: But how could this be? They're all in there walking around as free men, and the fourth looks like the Son of God.

REPORTER: Do you have a final statement you'd like to make to the press?

NEBUCHADNEZZAR: How's this? *(He grabs the microphone from* REPORTER.*)* I, King Nebuchadnezzar, do hereby make a new decree! Anyone caught speaking against the God of Shadrach, Meshach, and Abednego will immediately be destroyed, for there is no god more powerful than their God! *(He hands the microphone back to* REPORTER, *then walks toward the furnace as if to shut it off.)*

REPORTER *(as though into camera)*: And so, as King Nebuchadnezzar frees the prisoners, we conclude our report. But may we never forget the lesson we've all learned here today—the God of Shadrach, Meshach, and Abednego is a God who'll never leave you *(glances toward furnace)* . . . even when things get a little heated! And now back to our studios.

*(Blackout.)*

# The Catch of a Lifetime

## A sketch about the overflowing fishing nets

**Characters:**
 LARIUS
 URIAH

**Setting:**
 A fishing boat on the Sea of Galilee

**Props:**
 Fishing net
 A small sardine

**Costume:**
 Fishermen's wear from the Bible times


*(Sketch opens with* LARIUS *and* URIAH *in the boat. They're busy pulling up the net, anxious to view their catch.)*

LARIUS *(disappointed):* I can't believe this! We've been out here all night and all day, and this . . . *(he pulls an anemic sardine from the net and holds it up)* . . . is all we've got to show for it!

URIAH: And he's the *big* one. We threw the others back!

LARIUS: So, what do you suppose it is that's keeping the fish away?

URIAH: Hey, don't look at me. I showered this morning! *(Thinks for a moment.)* . . . Or was that yesterday morning?

LARIUS: Well, I guess we shouldn't feel too bad.

URIAH: Yeah. Some fishermen don't shower for weeks.

LARIUS *(gives him a look):* I mean, it looks as though none of the other fishermen have caught anything either.

URIAH: What about that one boat this morning? They pulled up a real beauty in their net.

LARIUS: Yeah, but a chariot wheel is a little hard to filet. *(Looking off to side)* Hey, wait a minute! What's going on over there in Peter's boat?

URIAH *(looking in same direction):* It appears that Man, Jesus, is telling him to take his boat out farther and lower his nets again.

LARIUS: But Peter's been out here for as long as we have. He knows there just aren't any fish to be caught today.

URIAH: If Jesus told me to do it, I think I'd do it, too.

LARIUS: You believe in this Prophet?

URIAH: I know there's something about Him. Something different.

LARIUS: Divine?

URIAH *(looking off toward Peter's boat again):* Look! They've done as Jesus said, and now their nets are overflowing. I've never seen so many fish!

LARIUS: So, where were all those fish when *we* were over there?

URIAH: Apparently, waiting for the Master's nets.

LARIUS *(looking at sardine):* So now, what do we do with him? He looks pretty puny compared to their catch.

URIAH: We could throw him back.

LARIUS: Naw. A guppy might eat him.

URIAH: Well, what do you say we have him mounted?

LARIUS: Mounted? Why, he'd get lost on a toothpick!

URIAH: Maybe, but every time we look at him, we'll be reminded of this day.

LARIUS: The day we didn't catch a thing?

URIAH: No. The day our hearts caught a glimpse of the Messiah.

*(Blackout.)*

# Forgive Us Our Debts

## A sketch about the unmerciful servant

**Characters:**
>KING
>HEBOAB
>SALOAM
>SOLDIER

**Setting:**
>City streets, Bible times

**Props:**
>Scroll

**Costumes:**
>Bible era clothing
>KING should have scroll tucked away inside his coat

*(Sketch opens as the KING walks onto stage. HEBOAB enters from the opposite direction.)*

KING *(to HEBOAB):* You. Come here.

HEBOAB *(looking around nervously):* Who? Me, O King?

KING: Don't you and I have some unfinished business to discuss?

HEBOAB *(gulps and walks over nervously):* Uh . . . you mean about that 10,000 talents I owe you?

KING *(sarcastic):* No, I mean about my chances for getting on Star Search! . . . Of course, I mean about that 10,000 talents you owe me. Now pay up or it's curtains for you!

HEBOAB: We just put in miniblinds, but thanks anyway. *(Tries to slink away.)*

KING *(grabbing hold of his collar to jerk him back in place):* Look, if you don't give me the money this instant, I'll be forced to sell you, your wife, and your children.

HEBOAB: You can't sell my wife and children.

KING: Why not?

HEBOAB: I tried that already. Fourteen people wanted their money back. But listen, I'm good for the money, I just need a little more time.

KING: Why is it every time I ask you about this money, you've got some excuse?

HEBOAB: At least I'm consistent.

KING: So, what is it *this* time?

HEBOAB: Bad investments. I guess the world just wasn't ready for designer loincloths.

KING: So, you don't have my money?

HEBOAB: Just give me a few more weeks. I promise I'll have it.

KING: Out of the question! I've waited long enough! Now there's only one thing left to do! (*He reaches into his coat and starts to pull something out, but we don't see it.*)

HEBOAB (*falling to the ground, pleading*): No! No! I'm too young to die! I'll get the money, I promise! Just give me another chance! Please! Please! I beg you! Don't kill me! Think how this will look in the news! Think how this will look to your subjects! Think how this will look on my credit rating!

KING: I'm not going to kill you.

HEBOAB: But isn't that a weapon in your coat?

KING (*pulling scroll from inside coat*): Only if I want to paper-cut you to death. This is just a document that says I'm forgiving you of your debt.

HEBOAB (*getting up, slightly embarrassed*): I knew that.

KING: Here. (*Hands him the scroll.*) Your slate has been wiped clean.

HEBOAB: You mean I don't owe you anything?

KING: Not a thing.

HEBOAB: Not even interest? (KING *shakes his head.*) But how can I ever thank you?

KING: By passing along this kindness to someone else. (KING *exits.*)

HEBOAB (*to himself*): I can't believe this! My entire debt has been forgiven! This is too good to be . . . (SALOAM *enters;* HEBOAB *spots him.*) Hey! I've been looking for you!

SALOAM (*nervously*): Oh, sir, if it's about that money I owe you, I promise I'll . . .

HEBOAB: Quit your sniveling, you parasite! I've had it with you and your lame excuses! You know, my good king just forgave me a huge debt and told me to pass along the kindness to someone else. But how can I do that when I've got to worry about flakes like you who owe me a measly 100 pence. Now pay up!

SALOAM: But, sir, I just don't have the money right now.

HEBOAB: Then how does jail sound to you?

SALOAM: But I've got a wife and kids.

HEBOAB: Hey, I'm not heartless. I'll tell them when visiting hours are.

(The KING *reenters.*)

KING (*to* HEBOAB): Oh, and one more thing . . . (*He notices* SALOAM.) Who's your friend?

HEBOAB: He's no friend, O King. Just a man who doesn't pay his debts. But don't worry. He's going to jail, then I can concentrate on passing along that kindness just like you said.

KING: Wait a minute! You're missing the point. I forgave you your debt. Why didn't you forgive this man his? That's the kindness I was talking about.

HEBOAB (*embarrassed*): I knew that. And that's exactly why this man is coming to my home for dinner! (*He puts his arm around him.*)

SALOAM: But I thought you said you were taking me to jail.

HEBOAB: Hey, my wife's a little possessive, but I wouldn't exactly call it jail.

KING (*to* HEBOAB): So, you really intended to send this man to prison for his debt?

HEBOAB (*laughing nervously*): A slight misunderstanding. That's all.

KING: Well, maybe you're right. Maybe jail *is* the answer.

HEBOAB: Then again, a prison sentence might do him some good!

KING (claps his hands, a soldier enters): Take the prisoner away!

HEBOAB: Yeah! Take the prisoner away!

(The SOLDIER takes HEBOAB by the arm and starts to escort him offstage.)

HEBOAB: Hey, wait a minute! Why are you taking *me?*

KING: You're being judged as you judged others.

HEBOAB: I am? Then I want a retrial!

KING: Sorry. The verdict's already been handed down . . . by you.

HEBOAB: I can't even appeal?

KING: Too late.

HEBOAB: But there must be something I can do!

KING: You could remember the next time you judge someone to go a little easier on them.

SALOAM: Yeah, after all, the sentence you hand out could very well end up being your own!

(As HEBOAB is led offstage by the SOLDIER, go to blackout.)

# The Foolish Builder
# (or)
# Why Is My Flat Flat?

---

## A sketch about the wise and foolish builders

---

**Characters:**
> WISE MAN
> FOOLISH MAN

**Setting:**
> A house built upon the sand. Its south wall should be leaning, its ceiling caving in, etc. The house should be able to collapse on cue.

**Props:**
> Various building tools

**Costumes:**
> Bible era or modern-day wear

*(Sketch opens with* FOOLISH MAN *busy working on his house, nailing things down, etc.* WISE MAN *enters.)*

WISE MAN: So, how's your house coming along?

FOOLISH MAN: See for yourself. I should have it done by nightfall. How 'bout yours?

WISE MAN: It's taking me a bit longer. I'm using a rock foundation, you know.

FOOLISH MAN *(laughs):* I know.

WISE MAN *(inspecting the house):* You used a sand foundation, didn't you?

FOOLISH MAN: How'd you guess?

WISE MAN: Most sunken living rooms don't drop down two stories.

FOOLISH MAN: Hey, no problem. A nail here, a nail there . . .

WISE MAN: And what about your patio?

FOOLISH MAN: What about it?

WISE MAN: It flew by my window this morning.

FOOLISH MAN: Yeah, well, you know those morning breezes. But not to worry, I'll have it back up in no time.

WISE MAN: I notice your south wall is leaning a bit.

FOOLISH MAN: That's part of the design. See, I'll hang all my pictures on my north wall. It'll balance out.

WISE MAN: And what about your roof? It appears to be caving in.

FOOLISH MAN: Hey, all houses do a certain amount of settling.

WISE MAN: A wrecking ball couldn't get it to do this much settling! You know what your problem is?

FOOLISH MAN: Yeah, my choice of neighbors!

WISE MAN: It's your foundation. A house is only as strong as its foundation.

FOOLISH MAN: Put that on a plaque and hang it in your den. I don't buy it.

WISE MAN: But it's true. It's obvious your house has nothing firm to stand upon. Why, the first storm that comes along will knock this baby down flat.

FOOLISH MAN: Nothing's gonna knock my house over! Why, it's as solid as a . . . (*He hits it, demonstrating its strength, but it falls over instead.*)

WISE MAN: You were saying?

FOOLISH MAN: I was saying . . . (*Bends over and gathers up a few pieces.*) . . . By any chance, is that rock next to you taken?

WISE MAN: It's all yours, neighbor! (*Puts his arm on FOOLISH MAN's shoulder and they walk offstage, smiling.*)

(*Blackout.*)

# A Talent Saved Is a Talent Lost

## A monologue about the slothful servant

**Character:**

SLOTHFUL SERVANT

**Setting:**

Outside a lord's home—Bible times

**Props:**

Pouch with coin inside

Mound of dirt

**Costume:**

Bible era clothing

*(Monologue opens with* SLOTHFUL SERVANT *awaiting his turn to report to his lord. The pouch is buried in the mound of dirt off to the side.)*

Oh, is my lord gonna be proud of me! Before he went away, he gave all of us here some talents. The guy in front of the line got five, the guy behind him got two, and I got one.

I didn't mind only getting the one since I tend to lose things anyway. That's why my chariot's still parked in the driveway after all these months. I can't find the keys! And that one summer I worked as a shepherd? I had to keep leaving the one to go find the 99!

Well, naturally, I didn't want to take any chances with my talent, so you know what I did? I buried it right here! *(He walks over to dirt mound and begins digging.)* See, this way I know it hasn't been lost, and it hasn't been stolen. . . . Unless, of course, a well-dressed gopher suddenly shows up on the scene!

*(He finds the pouch and lifts it up.)* Ah, here we go! *(He looks inside.)* It's perfect! Just as it was when I buried it here!

Now, there's nothing left to do but await my lord's praise.

But first, he has to take care of these two other fellows. And boy, are they in for it! I heard them say they actually went out and put their talents to use! Sure, they doubled what our lord gave them, but think of what they risked! I'd never do . . . *(Listens for a moment)* Wait a minute! My lord's telling them "Well done, thou good and faithful servant!"

Boy, if he calls *them* "good and faithful," I'll probably be inducted into the Servants Hall of Fame!

Ah, finally! *(He stands tall and puffs out his chest, proudly.)* It's my turn now!

*(To imaginary lord)* My lord, your talent is here just as you gave it to me. *(He holds out the pouch and bows, then adds)* And, lord, just a small banquet in my honor would suffice. I don't really go in for big . . .

. . . What's that? Me? A wicked and slothful servant? But my lord, you must be mistaking me for someone . . .

. . . What's that? You say you're going to give my talent to one of these other fellows because I never used it? . . . But, my lord, they've got so many already. Why would you . . . *(Obviously not getting anywhere)* . . . OK, OK, here it is. *(He sets the pouch down before him.)* I'm going. I'm going. *(He reluctantly starts to walk off, then stops and turns to audience.)*

Boy, oh, boy, I guess it's true what they say—bury your talent long enough and you'll end up without one! *(He exits, sulking.)*

*(Blackout.)*

# The Great Escape

---

## A sketch about Peter's escape from prison

---

**Characters:**
> ANNOUNCER
> GUARD NO. 1
> GUARD NO. 2

**Setting:**
> Prison, Bible times

**Props:**
> Two sets of chains (with wrist cuffs at the ends of each set)
> Hand-held microphone

**Costumes:**
> ANNOUNCER: May wear a suit
> GUARDS: Bible era clothing

*(Sketch opens with the guards standing just outside an empty prison cell. One set of chains should be attached to GUARD NO. 1's right wrist, and the other set is attached to GUARD NO. 2's left wrist. The opposite end of each chain is dragging the floor, quite obviously empty. ANNOUNCER, with microphone in hand, is standing off to the side. As he walks toward the guards, he looks toward the audience as if into camera.)*

ANNOUNCER: Good evening. We are here at the very prison cell from which Peter, a disciple of Christ, has just escaped.

GUARD NO. 1 *(quickly)*: He didn't escape. We've just, uh, misplaced him.

GUARD NO. 2: Temporarily.

ANNOUNCER: But I thought he slept chained between you two guards every night.

GUARD NO. 1: So? A lot of prisoners walk in their sleep.

ANNOUNCER *(examining the chains)*: But how could Peter have broken out of these heavy chains?

GUARD NO. 2: Hey, you'd do it, too, if you heard me snore. What's your point?

ANNOUNCER: My point is, Herod had special plans for this prisoner, Peter. You should have been keeping a closer eye on him.

GUARD NO. 2: Look, Peter was chained between us, there were extra guards posted all around, and there's a heavy iron gate out front. What more could we do?

ANNOUNCER: So then, you admit he's escaped?

GUARD NO. 1 (to GUARD NO. 2): Uh . . . can I see you for a moment?

GUARD NO. 2: Sure.

GUARD NO. 1 (backs away a few feet): Over here.

GUARD NO. 2 (walks over to him): Here?

GUARD NO. 1 (indicating ground right next to him): Here.

GUARD NO. 2 (moves over right next to him): Here?

GUARD NO. 1: Perfect. (Stomps on GUARD NO. 2's foot.) What's the matter with you?!

GUARD NO. 2 (rubbing his foot): You mean besides the excruciating pain in my foot?

GUARD NO. 1: Don't you realize we could lose our heads over this?

GUARD NO. 2 (sighs): Whew! For a minute there I thought you were going to say we could lose our jobs! (Suddenly realizing what GUARD NO. 1 said.) Wait a minute! Did you say we could lose our heads? (GUARD NO. 1 nods) But I'm still using mine!

GUARD NO. 1: That's a matter of opinion.

GUARD NO. 2: But it's not our fault an angel came and rescued Peter. Why should we be punished?

GUARD NO. 1: I know. We can't be expected to keep man in prison when his God has a spare key.

ANNOUNCER: Excuse me, but may we continue with the interview?

GUARD NO. 1 (aside to GUARD NO. 2): Let me handle this. (He walks back over to ANNOUNCER.) Sir, as we said before, Peter is around here someplace. We just can't seem to find him right now. But if you care to leave your card, we'll be happy to notify you as soon as he turns up.

ANNOUNCER: But . . .

GUARD NO. 1 *(leading him offstage)*: Good day.

GUARD NO. 2 *(after* ANNOUNCER *is gone)*: Whew! We finally got rid of him! But now what do we do?

GUARD NO. 1: That's easy. We start thinking like Peter.

GUARD NO. 2: I get it. We ask ourselves where would we hide if we were him.

GUARD NO. 1: No, I mean we really start thinking like him. We find out more about this God of his and start believing in Him just like Peter. After all, it sounds like this God of his is a God worth getting to know! (GUARD NO. 2 *nods in agreement as they walk offstage together.*)

*(Blackout.)*

# The Party Pooper

## A sketch about the prodigal son

**Characters:**
> FATHER
> SON

**Setting:**
> An upper room in the FATHER's house

**Props:**
> None needed

**Costumes:**
> Bible era clothes

*(Sketch opens with the SON, who is the prodigal son's brother, pouting in the corner. FATHER approaches.)*

FATHER: The party's downstairs. Why are you up here all alone?

SON: I don't feel much like partying.

FATHER: You're not happy your brother came home?

SON: Of course, I'm happy. I'm not *(dramatic)* "kill the fatted calf" happy, *(more subdued)* but I'm happy.

FATHER: My son, your brother has finally returned to us! Come, let us rejoice together! *(Holds out his hand in invitation.)*

SON: But, Father, he went away on his own accord.

FATHER: I know.

SON: He squandered his entire inheritance!

FATHER: . . . And his college fund.

SON: He came home smelling of pigs!

FATHER: That could have been a new cologne.

SON: Father, admit it. He hasn't acted like much of a son.

FATHER: He is still my son.

SON: But *I'm* the one who stayed here. *I'm* the one who took care of you.

FATHER: Don't you think I know that?

SON: Then why are you giving *him* the party? Shouldn't the cake have *my* name on it? Shouldn't *I* be the one opening all the gifts? Shouldn't the guests be singing that *I'm* a jolly good fellow?

FATHER: Son, if I rejoice in your brother's return, that doesn't mean I love you any less.

SON: It doesn't?

FATHER: No. You are my son. All that I have is yours. But he is my son also. And now, that part of my heart I thought I'd lost has been returned to me. Can't you understand my joy?

SON (*thinks for a moment, then smiles*): I think I can, Father.

FATHER: Then, come, join my party! (*Puts his arm around* SON *as they start to exit.*) Both of my sons are home where they belong. I have much to rejoice about! I have much to rejoice about!

(*Blackout.*)

# A Tale of Two Prayers

## A sketch about the Pharisee and the publican

**Characters:**
> PHARISEE
> PUBLICAN

**Setting:**
> Inside temple

**Props:**
> None needed

**Costumes:**
> Bible era clothing in accordance with character

*(Sketch opens with* PHARISEE *and* PUBLICAN *standing in the temple praying.* PHARISEE *holds his head up high and proud as he prays.* PUBLICAN *bows his head humbly as he prays.)*

PHARISEE: God, I thank Thee that I am not as other men are—liars, cheats, evil-minded, unjust, wrongdoing, low-life, or worse yet, like that publican over there probably is. *(He glances toward* PUBLICAN.*)*

PUBLICAN: God, be merciful to me a sinner.

PHARISEE *(under his breath)*: See, what'd I tell ya? *(He moves away from the* PUBLICAN *a few feet, then continues his prayer.)* And, Lord, I thank Thee that I can hold my head high when I talk to You . . . not like others of us in this room. *(He glances toward* PUBLICAN *again.)*

PUBLICAN: I am humbled in Your presence, Lord. Be merciful to me, a sinner.

PHARISEE: Of course, Lord, You know that I fast twice a week—You've no doubt read my bumper sticker. And You know I give tithes of all I possess—how could You miss reading about that on the billboard I rented? But, Lord, I just want to say that that's not half of what all I do for Your kingdom. Sure, the completed list will soon be printed up on fliers, but I figured it'd be a good idea to bring it up now.

PUBLICAN: Thank You, Lord, for salvation that doesn't come by works but by Your grace.

PHARISEE: Yes, Lord, if only the rest of the world were as righteous as I. Why, sometimes my goodness even surprises *me!*

PUBLICAN: Lord, Your goodness is immeasurable

PHARISEE: And finally, Lord, I want to thank Thee for hearing my prayers even in spite of all the *(looks toward* PUBLICAN*)* noise going on around me.

PUBLICAN *(to* PHARISEE*)*: Say, haven't you ever heard "the first shall be last and the last shall be first"?

PHARISEE: No. Are they a new singing group?

PUBLICAN: It's one of God's truths. It means those who exalt themselves will be abased and those who humble themselves will be exalted.

PHARISEE: You mean, someone like you can actually end up being exalted over someone like me? (PUBLICAN *nods his head and smiles broadly.)* You're kidding? (PUBLICAN *shakes his head and smiles broadly.)* Well, then, there's only one thing for me to do.

PUBLICAN: What's that?

PHARISEE: Get some of that . . . What do you call it?

PUBLICAN: Humility?

PHARISEE: Yeah, that's it. Can I get that around here, or do I have to send away for it?

PUBLICAN: There's only one place to get humility. And that's from in here. *(He points to his heart.)*

PHARISEE: You mean like . . . *(Bows his head reverently and prays.)* God, be merciful to me a sinner.

PUBLICAN: That's a good start.

PHARISEE: Hey, and it didn't even hurt a bit. Amazing, isn't it? What'd you call this again?

PUBLICAN: Humility.

PHARISEE: I kinda like it. It's me, you know what I mean?

PUBLICAN: And it's a much better you.

PHARISEE: Yeah. Thanks. *(As he exits)* And to think all these years I've been pushing to get to the front of the line when it's really the end of the line that's going to be first!

*(Blackout.)*

# The Weather Report

---

## A monologue about Jesus calming the storm

---

**Character:**

Weatherman Max Fitzgerald

**Setting:**

Newsroom

**Props:**

Desk

Chair

Facsimile of a teletypewriter

Several pieces of paper

**Costume:**

Suit

*(Monologue opens with* Max *sitting in the chair behind the desk. The teletypewriter is to his side. The papers are in front of him as he reads the latest weather report to his viewers.)*

Good evening. A severe storm warning has just been issued for the Sea of Galilee. Fishing vessels are advised to use extreme caution. The waters are rough, and many vessels have already capsized.

Again, we have a severe storm warning issued for the Sea of Galilee.

*(The teletypewriter begins receiving a message. He pulls it off and reads it.)* This just in! All boats on the Sea of Galilee are now instructed to return to shore until further notice. The storm is too great to ever survive. I repeat, if you are caught out there in the storm, you are being instructed to turn back at once!

We hope to have some numbers for you soon concerning the speed of winds, the size of the waves, and how long this storm is expected to last, but until then, just suffice it to say that this is one of the severest storms this meteorologist has ever covered.

*(Another message comes over the teletypewriter. He reads it.)* Ladies and gentlemen, we have just received word that a boat carrying several disciples, and the Master himself, is still out there on the turbulent waters. We

57

have tried to contact the vessel to advise them of the danger they're in, but all efforts thus far have been unsuccessful. We'll keep you posted.

*(Another message comes in over the teletypewriter. He reads it.)* Several witnesses have now reported that they saw this Man Jesus stand up in the boat and say three words, "Peace, be still."

Our researchers are checking this out now to see what the significance of these three words might be. Be assured we'll let you know just as soon as . . .

*(Another message comes in over the machine. He looks it over, then . . .)* Ladies and gentlemen! We have just had a most amazing turn of events! Word has just reached us that the storm that threatened the safety of all those on the Sea of Galilee is now over. The winds have died down and the sea is calm once again. Our storm warning is now lifted, and the sea is safe for all vessels!

And so, this is Max Fitzgerald saying good-night, and may we always remember what we've learned here today. A storm is only a storm until Jesus steps on the scene!

*(Blackout.)*

Mr. Robert Lund
9605 Glenarm Ct
Burke, VA  22015